Hush, Puppies

Hush, Puppies

CAROLRHODA BOOKS – MINNEAPOLIS

by BARBARA MITCHELL

pictures by
CHERIE R. WYMAN

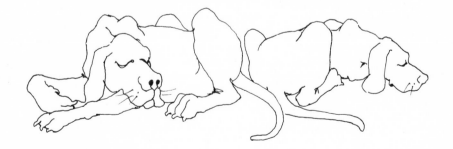

The recipe for Hush Puppies that appears on page
47 is taken from *Charleston Receipts*, compiled and
edited by the Junior League of Charleston (South
Carolina), Inc. Used by permission.

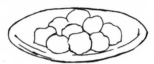

LIBRARY OF CONGRESS CATALOGING IN PUBLICATION DATA

Mitchell, Barbara, 1941-
    Hush, puppies.

    (A Carolrhoda on my own book)
    Summary: On a plantation in the South Carolina low
country during pre-Civil War times, a slave cook's
efforts to quiet barking hounds during a fish
fry results in hush puppies, which have been served at
fish fries ever since.
    [1. Cookery, American — Fiction. 2. United States —
Social life and customs — 1783-1865 — Fiction]
I. Wyman, Cherie R., ill. II. Title. III. Series.
PZ7.M686Hu 1983   [E]   82-4465
ISBN 0-87614-201-3

1 2 3 4 5 6 7 8 9 10 91 90 89 88 87 86 85 84 83

A Note from the Author

This story is based on the hush puppy legend. It comes to us from the South Carolina low country. In the days of the old south, plantation fish fries were popular. Hound dogs always came along with their owners. But the hounds were a problem. As soon as they smelled the fish cooking, they began to howl.

According to legend it was a slave cook who found a way to hush the puppies. Slaves invented many delicious recipes that we now call "soul food." But they gave us more than good food. We remember them especially for the great pride they took in their work and for the rich African heritage they handed down to us.

The plantations and people in this story are fictional. The slave names are names brought from West Africa. The low country slaves never stopped using the "day names" that reminded them of their homeland.

to my family —Walt, Wendy,
and Frieda (our Hush Puppy)
        -Barbara Mitchell

to Glenn and Annabelle
        -Cherie Wyman

Juba was the best plantation cook
in all of Carolina.
Her loaf bread was the lightest.
Her rice waffles were dainty as lace.
Secret spices,
brought from Africa long ago,
made her chicken and rice just right.

"Haven't I been cookin'
for Quiet River Plantation
since I was a child?"
she said proudly.
"And Mama Phibbi before me,
and Grandma Tamah before her?"

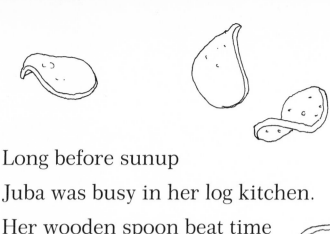

Long before sunup
Juba was busy in her log kitchen.
Her wooden spoon beat time
to the mockingbird's song
as she whipped up a fine breakfast
for Master Ben and Miss Sally.

Then Cuffee,
Juba's boy-child-born-on-a-Friday,
rang the breakfast bell.
And Quashee,
Juba's girl-child-born-on-a-Sunday,
rushed the platters of food,
hot as hot,
over to the Big House.

The Quiet River hounds
followed close behind.
Master Ben's Black-and-Tans
looked longingly at Juba's good food.
But they didn't beg.
They didn't make a sound . . .

11

. . . except for Bugler.
Bugler had the loudest voice
of all the Quiet River hounds,
and it seemed like he
was always howling.
Master Ben's other hounds
howled when they smelled fox.
Juba and Cudjo's hounds
howled at 'possum and 'coon.
But Bugler howled at things
like old hoes and cabbage leaves.

Quashee never got more
than halfway 'round the table
with Juba's hot corn bread
before Bugler let out a loud
"Er-oo! Er-oo!"

13

But in spite of Bugler,
Quiet River Plantation
was known to be a quiet place.
Foxes ran soundlessly
through the tall pines.

Catfish swam silently
in the still waters.
And all around was the gentle hush
of the quiet river rolling by.

Quiet River was a busy place too.

The Carolina low country

was rice country.

Master Ben was a rice planter.

Growing rice was hard work.

Slaves spent long, long days

planting and hoeing in the Carolina sun.

When summer came,

the days grew still and steamy.

The rice plants shimmered

in waves of heat.

Mosquitoes hung over the soggy fields,

spreading the Fever.

Master Ben and Miss Sally

left for their house in Charleston.

But the slaves had to keep right on working.

By fall the rice was plump and golden.

The days turned crisp and cool.

Master Ben and Miss Sally came home.

It was time to harvest the rice.

When the work was done at last,

Master Ben declared a holiday.

"Catfish time!"

the tired slaves shouted.

They all went down to the river.

All except Juba.

"Humph!" she said.

"They're sure to come back

with strings o' cats.

Master Ben will put up that flag.

And that'll mean cookin'

and more cookin'.

Call *that* a holiday?"

She got right down to making pies.

First came the sweet potato pies.

Then came the lemony buttermilk pies.

"Cookin' for all those folks,"

Juba muttered.

"And what thanks will I get?"

But by late afternoon
the pies were set to cool.
Juba set out to go fishing.
"Anyone knows catfish bite best
at sunset," she said.
Juba came back
with the biggest string of all.

Sure enough,
Master Ben rode out
to the end of his lane
the next morning.
He put up the signal flag.
All the other planters
knew just what that flag meant:
FISH FRY!

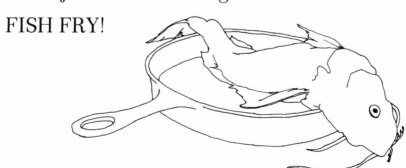

The news went up and down the river.

Everybody heard.

Everybody came.

And every planter brought his hounds.

Tall Oaks Plantation

brought their gentle Redbones.

Three Winds Plantation

brought their beautiful Blueticks.

Ricelands Plantation

brought their Walkers.

And, of course,

the Quiet River hounds were there.

The planters and their hounds
spent all day fox hunting.
The ladies got their party dresses ready.
"Party dresses indeed!" Juba mumbled
as she made batches and batches
of her best beaten biscuits
and crocks and crocks
of her Carolina cole slaw.

The children headed straight
for Juba's kitchen.
"Tell us some stories," they begged.
"Make us a johnnycake."

"Stories!
Johnnycake!
You think I got time for stories?"

"Ah, Juba . . ."

"Well . . ."
She got out the johnnycake board.
"Did I ever tell you the one
'bout Rabbit and Wolf at the dance?"

26

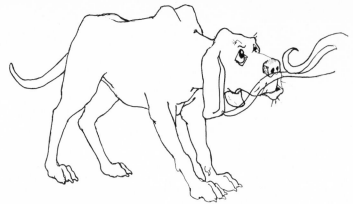

Soon the johnnycake

was browning nicely by the fire.

It sent out a mouth-watering aroma.

"Er-oo! Er-oo!"

Bugler again.

"Crazy hound," Juba said.

"Why aren't you out chasin' a fox?

Now *all* of you run along.

I've got a fish fry to get ready!"

Cudjo set up tables under the oaks.

He laid a great wood fire.

Over it he hung

a big, black kettle full of fat.

Then he skinned the "cats."

Juba dipped them in her special batter

By the time the planters got back,

the catfish were bubbling and sizzling

in the hot fat.

The planters and their hounds
all lay down by the fire.
The sweet smell of catfish frying
filled the air.
Banjo players strummed a soft tune.
There was hardly another sound.
Just the crackling of the fire
and the quiet river rolling by.
"There's nothing like the peace
of Quiet River Plantation,"
said the planter from Tall Oaks.

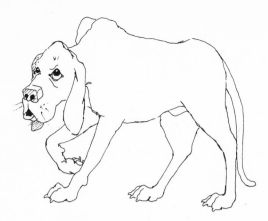

At that very moment

Bugler began to howl.

"Now what is that hound hollering about?"

Master Ben wondered.

It was embarrassing.

He looked at Bugler sternly.

But Bugler didn't stop.

Soon the Redbones joined him,
"Ah-oo, Ah-oo,"
with voices sweet as honey.
The Tall Oaks planter
gave them the quiet sign.
But they paid no attention.

Then the Blueticks started to sing,
"Oooh! Oooh!"
"Get the hounds some water,"
the Three Winds planter said.
But the hounds did not want water.
They kept right on howling.

Now the Walkers began to bellow.

"Owll! Owll!"

"Stop the banjos," Master Ben ordered.

"The music must hurt their ears."

So the banjo players stopped strumming.

But the hounds did not stop howling.

Juba nodded to Master Ben.
The fish were ready.
"No use tryin' to serve up a fish fry
in this racket," she muttered.
"That's two days' work all for nothin'."

Just then
the Quiet River Black-and-Tans,
the best-behaved hounds of all,
started in.
Their big, deep voices
were louder than all the rest.
"AWOO! AWOO!"

The Redbones crooned.

The Blueticks bawled.

The Walkers yowled.

The Black-and-Tans boomed.

The ladies looked sideways

at one another.

"*This* is Quiet River Plantation?"

The planters were disgusted.

"QUIET!" they yelled all at once.

But the howls came louder and faster,

till the hounds were all howling together

like a great hound-dog band—

with Bugler leading.

Master Ben looked at Juba:

Do something!

All this time
Juba had been watching,
and thinking too—
of old hoes . . .
and of cabbage leaves.
The slaves made hoe cakes at lunch time.
Hoe cakes were made with cornmeal.
Cudjo rolled ash cakes in cabbage leaves,
and ash cakes were made with cornmeal too.
Hoe cakes, ash cakes,
corn bread, johnnycakes.
All of those things
were made with cornmeal.
And catfish—
those catfish that were frying right now—
were dipped in cornmeal.

BUGLER HAD A NOSE FOR CORNMEAL!

Juba scooped up a spoonful
of her cornmeal batter
and dropped it into the hot fat.
It floated to the top,
puffed and golden.
She made a whole plateful.
Then she walked over to Bugler.
"Er—" he started to howl.
Juba popped a corn ball into his mouth.
"Now hush, puppy," she said softly.

Bugler's mouth closed.
He swallowed.
His tail wagged.
His mouth opened.
Not a sound came out.
In went another corn ball.

"Cuffee, Quashee," Juba called.
"Feed these to the hounds
while I make more."
So they tossed balls of cornmeal
to all the hounds.
And the hounds got as quiet as could be.

"Let me taste one of those things,"
said Master Ben.
He popped a golden morsel into his mouth.
Then he grinned.
"Hush Puppies for all!"
he ordered.

So the fish fry was served up
with plenty of Hush Puppies on the side.
Everybody ate those Hush Puppies
until they barely had room
for Juba's pies.
"Three cheers for Juba," they cried,
"the *best* plantation cook
in all of Carolina!"

The hounds were so full of Hush Puppies
that they all fell asleep by the fire.
The banjos strummed.
The hound dogs snored.
The river rolled quietly by.

And Hush Puppies have been served
at fish fries
ever since.

JUBA'S HUSH PUPPIES

2 cups cornmeal
1 teaspoon soda
1 teaspoon salt
6 tablespoons
  chopped onion

2 tablespoons flour
1 tablespoon baking powder
1 egg
2 cups buttermilk
red pepper to taste

Mix all dry ingredients. Add chopped onion, then milk and egg beaten together. Drop by small spoonfuls into boiling deep fat.* They will float when done. Drain on brown paper. Serve with fish. (Serves 8)

*Have a grown-up help you with the frying. Hot fat is dangerous.

Some Additional Information

page 7—Carolina is a term of endearment used
to describe both North and South
Carolina.
—A good loaf of bread was the true test
of a southern cook. Every plantation took
pride in its loaf bread.

page 16—Low country people living in hot, wet
places lived in fear of catching the Fever.
Today we call the disease Malaria.

page 26—"Rabbit and Wolf at the Dance" is an
old West African folktale.
—Johnnycakes were baked on a polished
board made of oak or hickory. The board
was tilted before the fire so that the
cake would brown.

pages 32-34—Each breed of hound has its own
sound. A hunter can identify the
different hounds by their voices.

page 38—Ash cakes were baked in the ashes on
the hearth. At special times the slaves
might bake a chicken wrapped in cabbage
leaves in the same way.